POEMS
BY
ME

Still Smiling While Fighting
Autoimmune Illnesses

Alys Perez Capozzi

FCP

Full Court Press
Englewood Cliffs, New Jersey

First Edition

Copyright © 2016 by Alys Perez Capozzi

Published in the United States of America
by Full Court Press, 601 Palisade Avenue,
Englewood Cliffs, NJ 07632
fullcourtpressnj.com

ISBN 978-1-938812-80-4

*Thanks to my mother for the art that appears
above the poem "Good Night"*

*Editing and book design by Barry Sheinkopf
for Bookshapers (bookshapers.com)*

Colophon by Liz Sedlack

THIS BOOK IS DEDICATED TO

my many friends who also deal
with the challenges
that confronted us on a daily basis,
and our families, who choose to stay
and support us with love.

Preface

I HAVE BEEN LIVING with multiple sclerosis since the delicate age of fifteen. That was only the beginning. If only that had also been the end of the illnesses I have had to endure! Unfortunately, more autoimmune diseases followed. Hence, I have had ever more challenges to confront.

Knowing there is only one way to succeed at living despite having these chronic diseases, though, I personally remind myself to be surrounded by people who emit positive energy. This is how I have been able to survive this hell on Earth.

Writing poems has been a way out. Oh, I have found others, but this is one. I hope my poems can encourage you to do something *you* have avoided because of fear that it won't be "good enough." Everyone needs to escape their troubles in life. This is one of mine. I know you can find yours! Quitting is not an option.

Table of Contents

MS & Me

I had to, Dear God, write to you.
I know it's been so long.
I had to write and tell you
I'm trying to be strong.

Today it's been a year now
since I was diagnosed.
Twelve months went by so quickly.
I'm trying still to cope.

These symptoms are so crazy,
sometimes I just can't walk.
The burning pain that's in my legs—
I want it just to stop.

The numbness is much better now,
the weakness has improved,
the bladder problems are no more. . .
so much I want to do.

I must be in remission.
How long I just can't tell.
It doesn't really matter—
I'm grateful just as well.

MS and me, we'll make it,

I know I must believe.
Please God, won't you please give me
all the strength I need?

Something About You

There's just something about you;
I don't know what it is.
Your kindness and sincerity
are just a part of it.

The thoughtfulness you show me
is really overdone.
I don't think I deserve it.
You always prove me wrong.

You're always there to listen
and give me good advice.
You never make false promises.
You never tell me lies.

You treat me like a lady,
you treat me like a friend,
you show me that you really care.
On you I can depend.

There's just something about you—
I gave it lots of thought.
I'm not sure if I'll ever know
what makes you special, Scott.

Nobody Told Me

Nobody told me.
I never knew
you my friend would be leaving me.
I had not a clue of my Lord's plan for you,
A twenty-three-day hospital stay?
No, it should not have been that way
as God guided you from up above,
fulfilling his plan With his trusting love.
"Time to come home," he said to you then.
Good-bye my friend, till we meet again.

The Journey

How do you know where to go?
Are you searching for answers
at end of the rainbow?
Was it what you expected
once you got there,
or do you think life is unfair?
Perhaps you've been looking
through rose-colored glasses,
hoping this bad time eventually passes.
Did you honestly think
you would never feel sorrow?
Did you really believe in
just happy tomorrows?
Not once were you told
that this would be easy
(that prediction you made on your own).
Seldom does life ever go as expected.
Find comfort in knowing that you're not alone.
I wish I could say that I have all the answers,
but, sadly, I can't say I do
All I can say
is I live day to day
Knowing eventually
I'll find the way.

The Give-Me Man

What is it you want?
asked the give me man.
What is it you want me to give?
Are you talking to me? I asked hastily.
Yes, of course, he responded without hesitation,
or even to notice my look of frustration.
I'm the Give-Me Man,
He continued to chatter.
Tell me what you want.
Tell me what's the matter.
My life is a-scatter,
That's what's the matter.
I've too many troubles, more than I can handle.
Then it's done, he said to me with such ease.
I'll destroy them all, if that's what you please.
But wait! No! You're much too kind.
You see, all I'm asking for is
peace of mind.

Precious

So sad it has to end this way.
I just don't know what else to say.
I tried to tell you how I feel,
but you just turn away.

So sad that we must say good-bye.
My love for you will never die.
If ever we should meet again,
I hope it is as friends.

Trophy

I'm so depressed.
I'm so distraught.
This isn't what I thought.

This isn't how my life should be.
This isn't what I planned for me.
I'm sick of being lonely.

I want to walk.
I want to dance.
Please, dear God,
give me one more chance.

I'll give it everything I've got.
Please just give me one more shot.
"Don't you stop being beautiful,"
my child tells me.

I smile at him gratefully.
He makes me smile.
He gives me hope.

So here I go.
I can't give up.
That's not the plan.

I know I can
believe in me,
believe that God can make it be.
So, stay with me, dear Lord.
Watch me be your trophy.

Worth

What's the payoff? What's it worth? Why do I bother being this way? Who benefits, anyway? Why do I bother treating others as I wish to be treated? I feel nothing but defeated, drained of the little energy I am left with, wasting my time explaining my actions as if I had bad intentions.

I feel sad and isolated. I feel life for me is over-rated— sitting here all alone with no one to talk to, just the computer and me, wanting desperately to move.

I wish I had a physical therapist to encourage me, to help me be the best me I can be physically. I wish my husband would just be my husband, there for me with love and support, doing whatever because he loves me, not resents me. You hurt me so. I know I don't deserve the way I am treated by this man, doing what I can, always. Why bother? It's never right, no matter what. The way he *talks* to me. Am I not his equal? Partner for life? I feel like I'm walking on eggshells around him, holding my breath until the next time he wipes that smile right off my face. He keeps it off. It doesn't matter to him. I don't matter to him. It doesn't matter what I say, it's the wrong thing anyway. It doesn't matter what I do, it's the wrong thing to you. I'm doing what I can to make this life livable. It's very hard, I won't deny, challenging at best. Realistically, it's up to me.

This is so *difficult*. I trust God finds me capable of dealing with it! I'm so tired, exhausted, fatigued. I feel as if it's hard work. . .just to breathe, waiting for things to turn my way.

Silly, I think—really, I'm okay.

Beautiful Child

Beautiful child growing up so fast,
I can't believe that years have passed.
No longer are you my little boy
but closer to the man you'll someday be.
What can I say but I like what I see,
so proud of you as you find your way through
life's many challenges every day.
While I constantly struggle to live
with this illness,
I look at you and am reminded
Of the beautiful child I've been blessed with.
So thank you for coming into my life:
I could not make it without you.
Thank You, God, for giving Tristian to me.
I pray he becomes the man
You want him to be.

The Letter Z

The letter Z, you'll find

resembles very much

a tipsy vertical line

turned upside down remains the same
but when turned sideways

it gains a whole new name.

Look At Me

Look at me
Do you really see me?
Do you see the real me?
Do you see God's love
guiding me through life
with a gentle touch of love
as I make choices
of how I want to live?
Do you see my love for you
as sincere and honest?
Your eyes look at me;
you decide how to treat me. . . .
Be wise.
Make smart decisions.
Your *son* needs you to show him
How to be a strong, intelligent man.
Your son just needs you.
I need you.
Be the father you strive to be,
the man you claim to be.

Remember

I remember going to church each Sunday,
big beautiful white building
with the steeple so high—
Sunday school as a two-year-old:
Jesus loves me
this I know,
for the bible
tells me so. . . .
I'll never forget the Chapel by the Lake
The many memories there,
from singing in the
choir as a child
to evening services there with singles,
I as a young adult.
I remember Dr. Jess Moody.
From him, I learned how to be a Christian.
That I will never forget
Thank you, my friend;
I will cherish these memories until the end.

What Next?

What next, I dare to contemplate
for fear that I might complicate
my situation, stable now, I think.
I'm feeling happy, strong, ready to face
whatever challenge comes.

Then this, this bump on my forearm:
It's painful, ugly. . .
but nothing like the way he treated me
yesterday, the way he does today.
So I pray.

Erase

I hurt outside,
I hurt inside.
It's painful everywhere.
I do not dare
express my feelings though,
disturb their peace,
don't want to let the others
feel my discomfort.
It's unbearable for most.
I'll keep it to myself, locked up inside.
I'll hurt alone, as I
do often do, tears running down my face.
This is the hurt I want to erase.

Crazy

My husband thinks I'm lazy
my son thinks I am crazy,
but I think I am me,
which is crazy mixed with dazy.

I will do my best
with crazy, dazy me.
I like me.
No negative thoughts allowed,
only happy to be me!

Hard To Be Me

It is hard to be me,
difficult to live this life.
At times it feels impossible
At times intolerable.
Each day I am not sure what to expect;
Each day I find a way
to make life work for me.
My choice,
my Life,
me.
It's hard to be
but I like me!

Confused

Confused, that's me!
I can't recall what day it is,
don't know the time.
I can't remember how to do
the thing I'm doing
I only know that I'll be fine
and shrug:
One day at a time.

Always

Always here for you, I'll always be—
always will support you, always will
encourage you, and you can count on that,
always trust you, trust you've earned,
always, Tristian, no matter what,
I'll always love you all the ways I know,
always.

Good Night

Good night, Mima. I hope you rest.
It's peaceful there at best.
I asked God to watch over you.
I know He will; he told me, too.
Give Papi a big kiss from me.
I know he's waited patiently.

I love you,
miss you,
wish I would have been with you
to hold your hand,
to say adios, Mima.
So hard for me to say, "Good-bye,"
so I'll just say. . .
"Good night."

Unexpected

Unexpected leaving us this way,
A life ending too soon.
Memories of being in your wedding,
Memories of you:
While our tears keep falling
I don't understand. What was His plan?
So we pray for God to show us.
Leaving us much too young,
showing us all that you've done.
Rest in peace, Matt,
Your mission is done here
Rest.

Wonderful

I was smiling until I showed you
my last poem.
Redundant?
I should not have shown it to you.
These are my words, only meant for me!
Don't judge me,
hurt me. I am like a delicate wildfire.
Your words, not mine.
I love you. These are my words to you.

Happy

Still happy but so busy!
Responsibility leads to independence.
Independence is what I want!
Independence is my goal.
I will independently continue with my hectic day,
happy.

Not About Me

I wake up each morning grateful
for another day—
stretching, moving, breathing,
another day,
thinking
how wonderful it would be
to be healthy and free
from these illnesses
for just one day.
Then I struggle with these thoughts
and this body
for this current day
because it's not about me—
my trials are invisible.
It's about all the other people
I speak to each day
you who are able to look away.
Don't look at me, not today.
So today I will make the most of my day,
making today about
me. . . .
Just today.

Broken

"We are all broken;
That's how the light gets in."

                                        —Anon.

I feel broken today—
only for now.
I feel as though my living
needs to rest.
I need a break
from the way I feel in your presence.
The way my dreams, my possibilities,
tomorrow's hopes,
all disappear.
I do not feel productive.
don't feel well,
not making the most of my time.
I feel broken.

Till Next Time

This book of poems is done for now,
my challenges complete,
but there'll be more encounters still—
I won't accept defeat.

www.ingramcontent.com/pod-product-compliance
Lightning Source LLC
Chambersburg PA
CBHW022349040426
42449CB00006B/785